UNDERSTAND YOUR
Mind AND Body

I0201612

Speech Disorders

AJ Knight

Explore other books at:
WWW.ENGAGEBOOKS.COM

VANCOUVER, B.C.

WWW.ENGAGEBOOKS.COM

Speech Disorders: Understand Your Mind and Body
Knight AJ -
Text © 2023 Engage Books
Design © 2023 Engage Books

Edited by: A.R. Roumanis, Ashley Lee,
Melody Sun and Sarah Harvey
Design by: Mandy Christiansen
Consultant: Heather Romero - Child
Youth and Family Counsellor

Text set in Montserrat Regular.
Chapter headings set in Hobgoblin.

This book is not meant to replace the advice of a medical professional or be a tool for diagnosis. It is an educational tool to help children understand what they or other people are going through.

FIRST EDITION / FIRST PRINTING

LIBRARY AND ARCHIVES CANADA CATALOGUING IN PUBLICATION

Title: Speech disorders / AJ Knight.
Names: Knight, AJ, author.
Description: Series statement: Understand your mind and body

Identifiers: Canadiana (print) 2023044699x | Canadiana (ebook) 20230447007
ISBN 978-1-77476-792-4 (hardcover)
ISBN 978-1-77476-793-1 (softcover)
ISBN 978-1-77476-794-8 (epub)
ISBN 978-1-77476-795-5 (pdf)
ISBN 978-1-77878-114-8 (audio)

Subjects:
LCSH: Speech disorders in children—Juvenile literature.
LCSH: Speech therapy for children—Juvenile literature.
LCSH: Speech disorders—Juvenile literature.

Classification: LCC RJ496.S7 K65 2023 | DDC J618.92/855—DC23

This project has been made possible in part by the Government of Canada.

Canada

Contents

What Are Speech Disorders?

Speech disorders affect how people talk. They might know what to say but have trouble making the right sounds. People of any age can have a speech disorder.

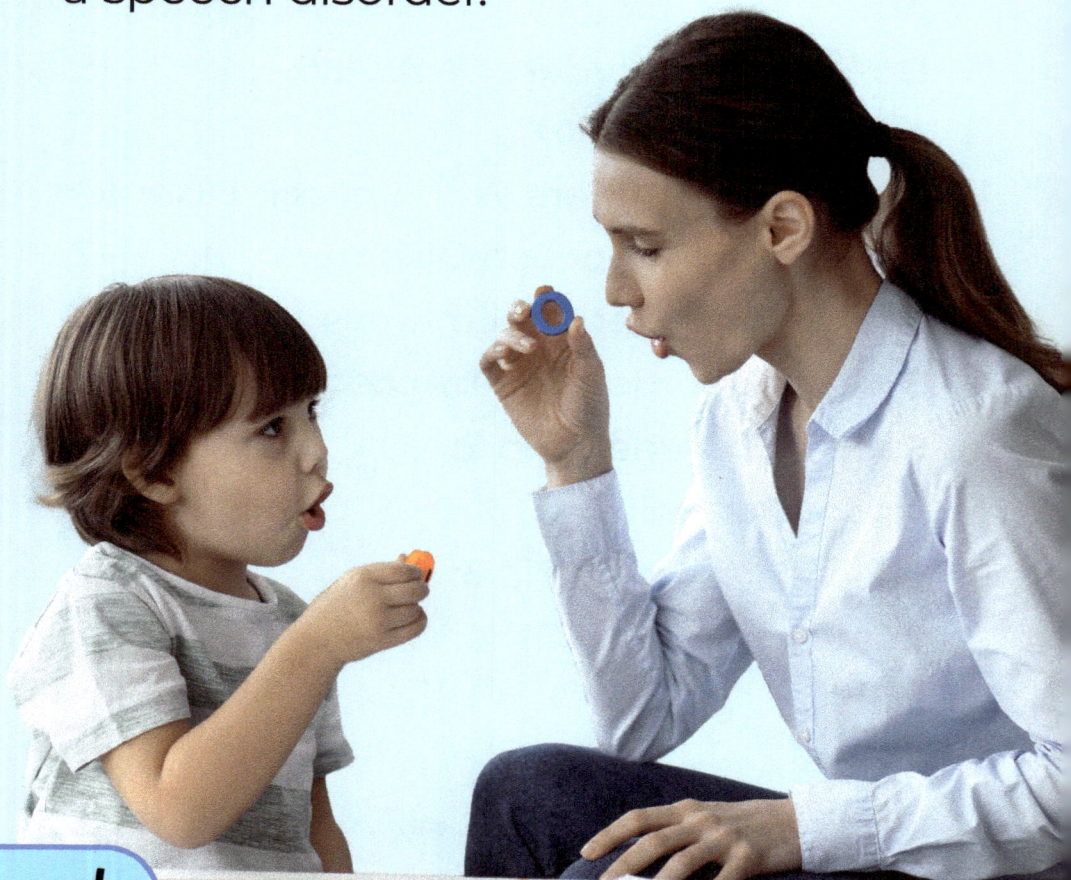

Many people mix up speech disorders with language disorders. People with a language disorder have trouble understanding what others mean and getting their own meaning across to others. People with speech disorders do not have trouble with this.

Some young children have both a speech disorder and a language disorder.

Kinds of Speech Disorders

There are many different kinds of speech disorders. Some people might have trouble saying sounds correctly. This can sometimes make it hard for others to understand them.

Some people with speech disorders may have a hard time speaking smoothly. One of the most common kinds of speech disorders is stuttering. People who stutter may start and stop talking many times. They might also repeat certain sounds or words.

"w-w-wa-want to g-g-go to the p-park park?"

What Causes Speech Disorders?

Some people are born with a speech disorder. These speech disorders may be passed down from parent to child. Others may happen as a person gets older.

Some speech disorders are caused by injuries. An injury is when someone's body gets hurt. Someone may get a speech disorder because of brain damage or hearing loss.

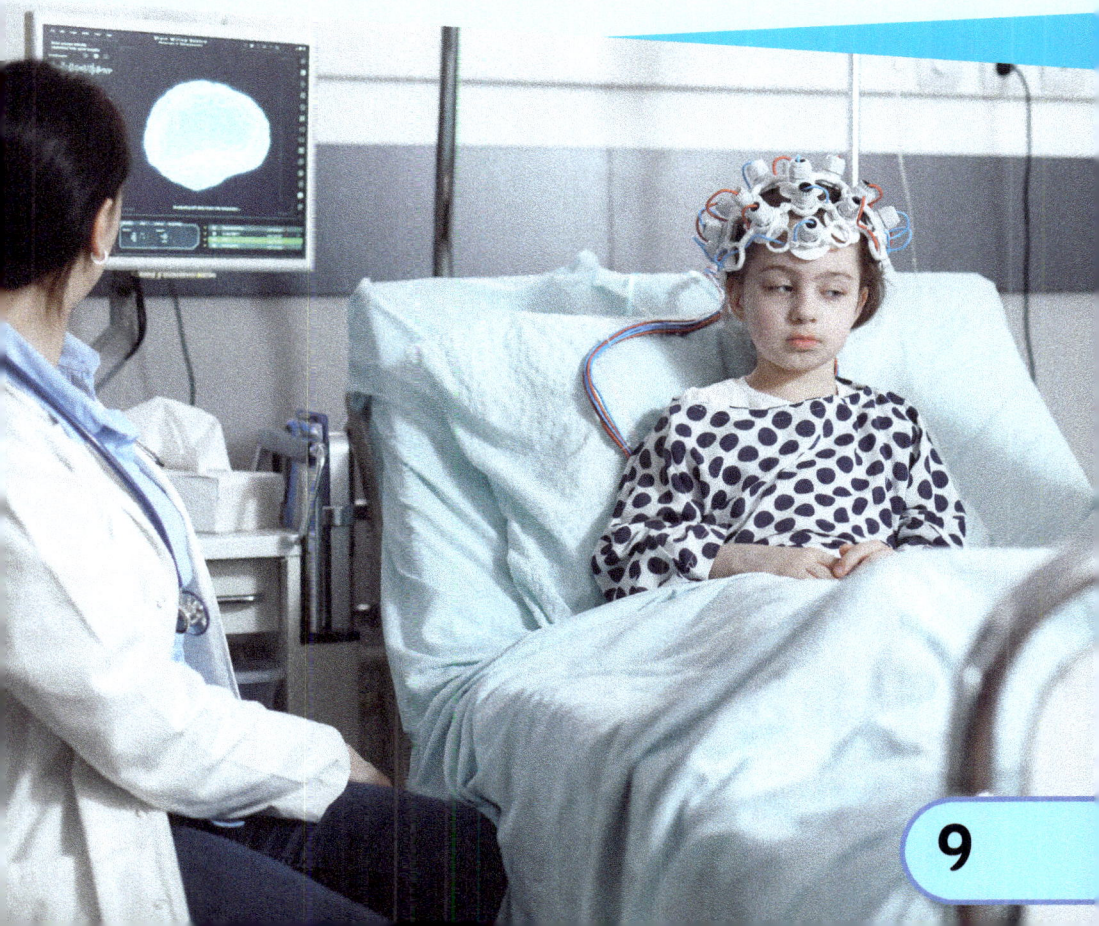

How Do Speech Disorders Affect Your Brain?

Speech disorders do not often have an effect on the brain. But the brain can have an effect on how a person speaks. Speech is mostly controlled by a part of the brain called the cerebrum. Damage to this area can sometimes cause a speech disorder.

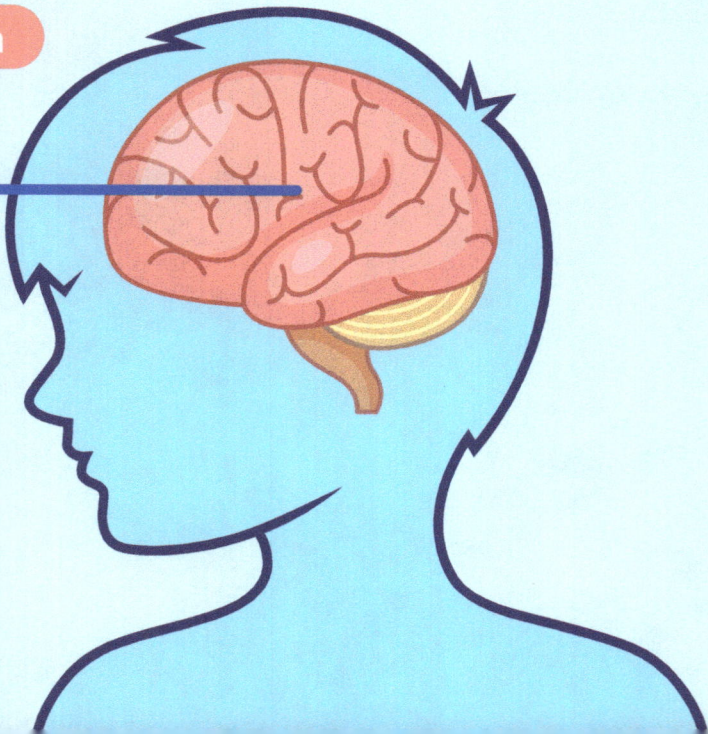

Cerebrum

Having a speech disorder can affect someone's mental health. They may feel bad about themselves or become embarrassed. Some people may get **anxiety**.

KEY WORD

Anxiety: feelings of worry and fear that are hard to control.

How Do Speech Disorders Affect Your Body?

Some people with speech disorders have trouble controlling parts of their mouth. They may not be able to get their tongue to do what they want. Sometimes the **muscles** in someone's mouth are not strong enough for them to speak clearly.

KEY WORD

Muscles: parts of the body that help people and animals move.

Some people have a speech disorder because part of their face is paralyzed. Being paralyzed means someone cannot move part of their body. This is often caused by an injury.

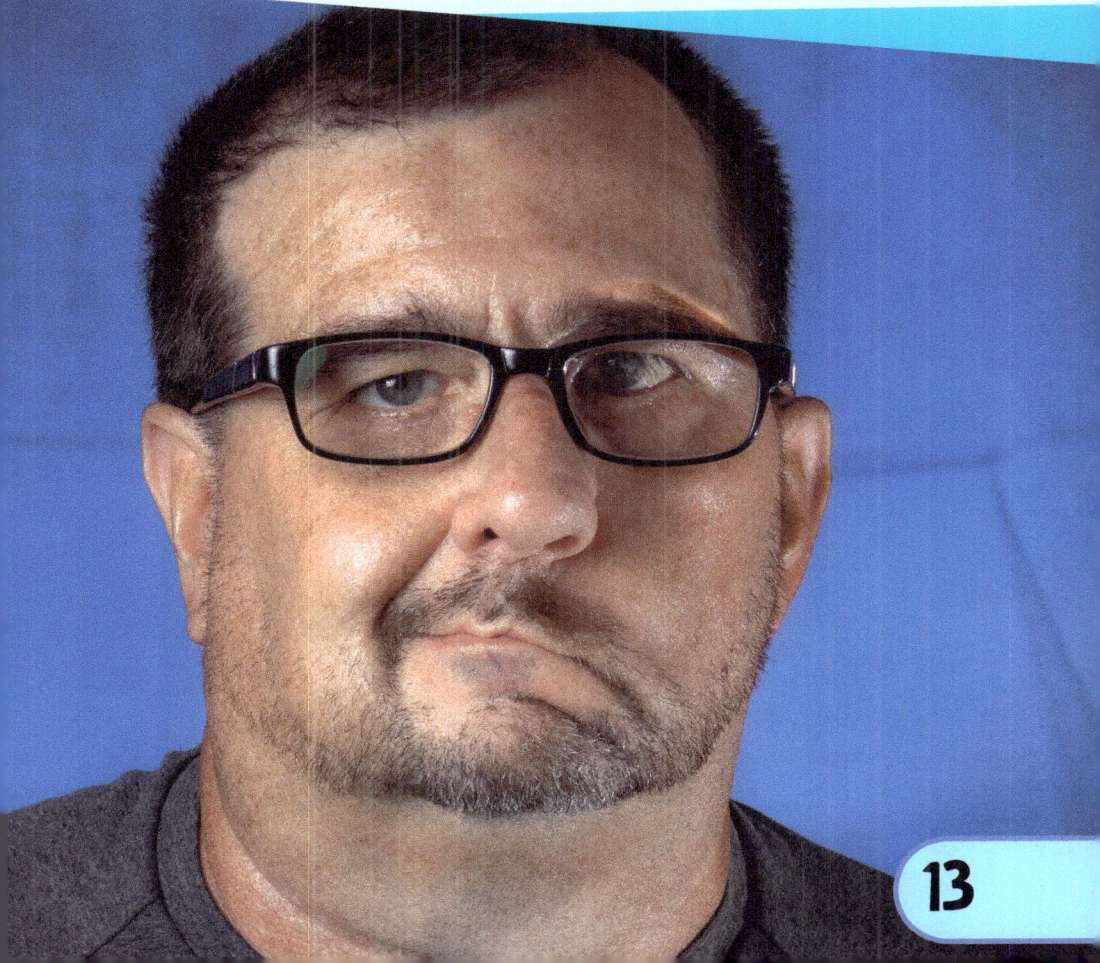

Do Speech Disorders Go Away?

Some speech disorders go away on their own. Others do not. Someone might have a speech disorder their whole life.

> While most kids with a stutter will outgrow it, about one out of four will stutter their whole life.

Some people with speech disorders might need the help of a speech therapist. Speech therapists are trained to help people with speech and language disorders. Speech therapists help people by talking with them, playing games, or giving them exercises.

Asking for Help

Asking for help can be scary. Find an adult that you feel comfortable talking to. There are many people who want to help!

"I know what word I want to say, but I can't make myself say it. Why do words feel like they're stuck in my throat?"

"I think I might have a stutter. How can I make it get better?"

"I feel like I say words wrong all the time. It makes me nervous in front of my friends. Is there someone I can talk to about it?"

How to Help Others With Speech Disorders

Reading this book and learning about speech disorders is a great first step in helping someone with a speech disorder. Understanding what they are going through will help you help them. Here are some more ways you can help.

Do not judge

Be respectful if someone tells you about their speech disorder. Be kind and do not judge them if they make mistakes. People with speech disorders are just as smart as everyone else.

Listen

People with speech disorders can be nervous to speak in front of others. Keep eye contact and nod so they know you are listening. What someone says is more important than how they say it.

Be patient

Give the person with a speech disorder time to speak. Try not to talk over them or guess the end of their sentence. Staying calm and relaxed can help them feel more comfortable.

The History of Speech Disorders

Samuel Potter was a doctor who had a stutter. He wrote one of the first American books about speech disorders in 1882. His book encouraged other doctors to do more to help treat speech disorders.

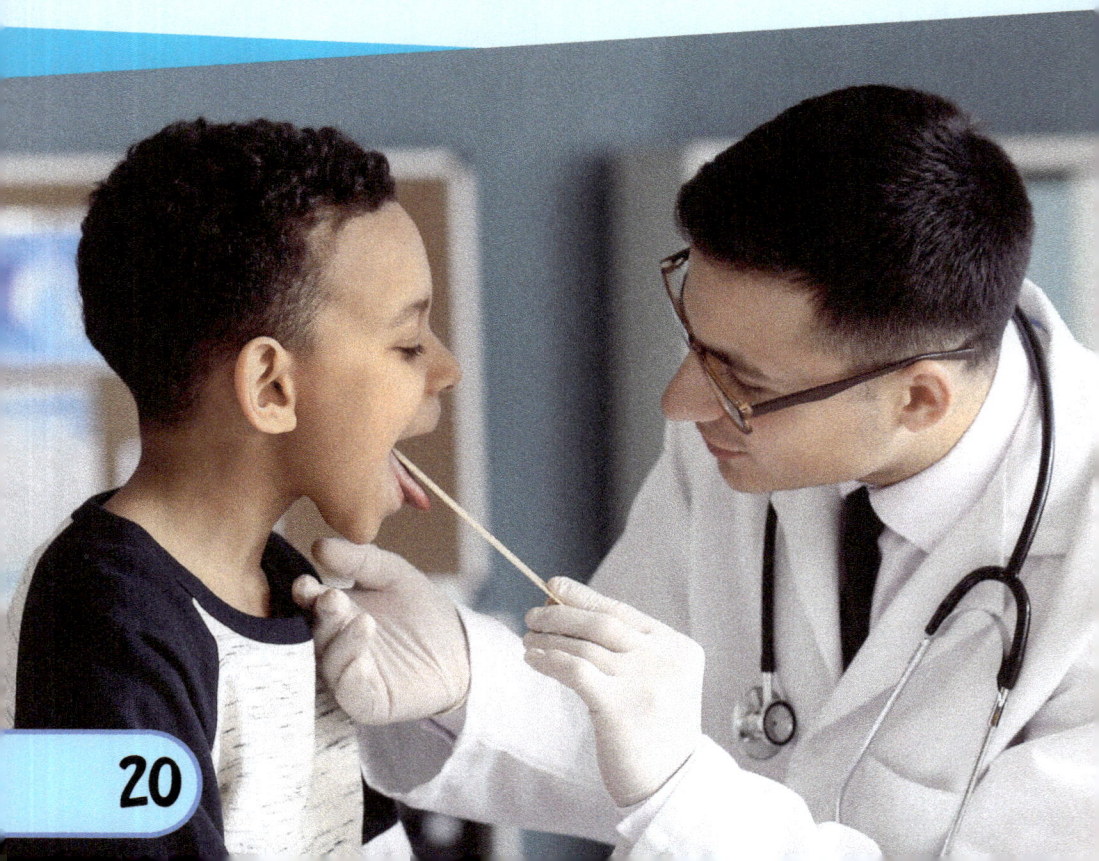

Sara Mae Stinchfield Hawk was a doctor who studied speech. She was one of the 25 people who started the American Speech and Hearing Association (ASHA) in 1925. In 2023, the ASHA had around 228,000 members.

Many soldiers came back from World War II with brain injuries that caused speech disorders. Because of this, people began to study how the brain affects speech. During this time, testing for speech disorders got better.

Speech Disorder Superheroes

Having a speech disorder does not have to stop you from doing things you love. Many people with speech disorders do great things. Check out these speech disorder superheroes who are open to sharing their experiences!

James Earl Jones was the voice of Darth Vader in the Star Wars movies. He became **non-verbal** as a child because his stutter made him nervous in front of others. Reading poetry out loud helped him work with his stutter.

KEY WORD

Non-verbal: unable to communicate by writing or talking.

Actor **Emilia Clarke** could not speak clearly after having two brain injuries. Her speech returned after a week, and she was able to continue acting. Emilia started a group called SameYou to raise money for people healing from injuries like hers.

Joe Biden gives many speeches as the President of the United States. He has worked his whole life to overcome his stutter. As a child, Joe practiced speaking clearly by reading poetry in front of a mirror.

Speech Disorders Tip 1: Accepting Yourself

There is nothing wrong with having a speech disorder. Making mistakes is a part of life. It is never okay for anyone to make you feel bad about it.

Find out what helps you feel more confident when you talk. Take a moment to plan what you are about to say. Some people find taking a few deep breaths and speaking slowly helps them.

Make sure to tell an adult if someone is mean to you.

Speech Disorders Tip 2: Asking for Help

Ask a friend or family member to practice talking together. Go over any words you find difficult. It might help to say the words while looking in a mirror or listen to them played back on a recording.

Ask an adult about finding a speech therapist. You and the speech therapist can work together to find what helps you. A **counselor** may also be helpful if you feel nervous talking in front of others.

KEY WORD

Counselor: a person who gives advice to others.

Speech Disorders tip 3: Connecting With Others

Many people around the world have a speech disorder. Try connecting with some of them! Building your own community can be a great way to share your experiences.

Friends, family, and classmates can all be part of your community. If you do not have anyone in your area, try looking for groups online. Ask an adult to help you find a speech disorder group for kids your age!

Quiz

Test your knowledge of speech disorders by answering the following questions. The questions are based on what you have read in this book. The answers are listed on the bottom of the next page.

1 What do many people mix up speech disorders with?

2 What is one of the most common kinds of speech disorders?

3 Can someone be born with a speech disorder?

4 What part of the brain is speech mostly controlled by?

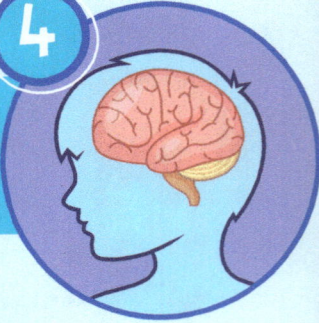

5 What are speech therapists trained to do?

6 Who wrote one of the first American books about speech disorders?

Explore Other Level 3 Readers.

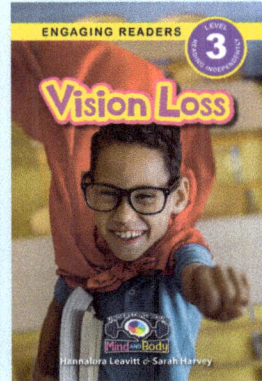

ADHD
ENGAGING READERS — LEVEL 3
AJ Knight

Anxiety
ENGAGING READERS — LEVEL 3
Adelaide Wilder

Asthma
ENGAGING READERS — LEVEL 3
Sarah Harvey

Body Image
ENGAGING READERS — LEVEL 3
Adelaide Wilder

Dyslexia
ENGAGING READERS — LEVEL 3
Sarah Harvey

Diabetes
ENGAGING READERS — LEVEL 3
Kit Caudron-Robinson

Hearing Loss
ENGAGING READERS — LEVEL 3
AJ Knight

Obesity
ENGAGING READERS — LEVEL 3
Kit Caudron-Robinson

Vision Loss
ENGAGING READERS — LEVEL 3
Hannalora Leavitt & Sarah Harvey

Visit www.engagebooks.com/readers

Answers:
1. Language disorders 2. Stuttering 3. Yes
4. The cerebrum 5. Help people with speech and
language disorders 6. Samuel Potter

www.ingramcontent.com/pod-product-compliance
Lightning Source LLC
Chambersburg PA
CBHW051240020426
42331CB00016B/3459